ANALYSIS

TASK CARD SERIES

Conceived and
written by
RON MARSON

Illustrated by
PEG MARSON

D1411195

TOPS LEARNING
SYSTEMS

10970 S Mulino Road
Canby OR 97013
Website: topscience.org
Fax: 1 (503) 266-5200

Oh, those pesky **COPYRIGHT RESTRICTIONS** *!*

Dear Educator,

TOPS is a nonprofit organization dedicated to educational ideals, not our bottom line. We have invested much time, energy, money, and love to bring you this excellent teaching resource.

And we have carefully designed this book to run on simple materials you already have or can easily purchase. If you consider the depth and quality of this curriculum amortized over years of teaching, it is dirt cheap, orders of magnitude less than prepackaged kits and textbooks.

Please honor our copyright restrictions. We are a very small company, and book sales are our life blood. When you buy this book and use it for your own teaching, you sustain our publishing effort. If you give or "loan" this book or copies of our lessons to other teachers, with no compensation to TOPS, you squeeze us financially, and may drive us out of business. Our well-being rests in your hands.

What if you are excited about the terrific ideas in this book, and want to share them with your colleagues? What if the teacher down the hall, or your homeschooling neighbor, is begging you for good science, quick! We have suggestions. Please see our *Purchase and Royalty Options* below.

We are grateful for the work you are doing to help shape tomorrow. We are honored that you are making TOPS a part of your teaching effort. Thank you for your good will and kind support.

Sincerely, Ron Marson

Purchase and Royalty Options:

Individual teachers, homeschoolers, libraries:

PURCHASE option: If your colleagues are asking to borrow your book, please ask them to read this copyright page, and to contact TOPS for our current catalog so they can purchase their own book. We also have an **online catalog** that you can access at www.topscience.org.

If you are reselling a **used book** to another classroom teacher or homeschooler, please be aware that this still affects us by eliminating a potential book sale. We do not push "newer and better" editions to encourage consumerism. So we ask seller or purchaser (or both!) to acknowledge the ongoing value of this book by sending a contribution to support our continued work. Let your conscience be your guide.

Honor System ROYALTIES: If you wish to make copies from a library, or pass on copies of just a few activities in this book, please calculate their value at 50 cents (25 cents for homeschoolers) per lesson per recipient. Send that amount, or ask the recipient to send that amount, to TOPS. We also gladly accept donations. We know life is busy, but please do follow through on your good intentions promptly. It will only take a few minutes, and you'll know you did the right thing!

Schools and Districts:

You may wish to use this curriculum in several classrooms, in one or more schools. Please observe the following:

PURCHASE option: Order this book in quantities equal to the number of target classrooms. If you order 5 books, for example, then you have unrestricted use of this curriculum in any 5 classrooms per year for the life of your institution. You may order at these quantity discounts:

2-9 copies: 90% of current catalog price + shipping.

10+ copies: 80% of current catalog price + shipping.

ROYALTY option: Purchase 1 book *plus* photocopy or printing rights in quantities equal to the number of designated classrooms. If you pay for 5 Class Licenses, for example, then you have purchased reproduction rights for any 5 classrooms per year for the life of your institution.

1-9 Class Licenses: 70% of current book price per classroom.

10+ Class Licenses: 60% of current book price per classroom.

Workshops and Training Programs:

We are grateful to all of you who spread the word about TOPS. Please limit duplication to only those lessons you will be using, and collect all copies afterward. No take-home copies, please. Copies of copies are prohibited. Ask us for a free shipment of as many current **TOPS Ideas** catalogs as you need to support your efforts. Every catalog contains numerous free sample teaching ideas.

ISBN 0-941008-80-0

CONTENTS

A TOPS Model for Effective Science Teaching...

If science were only a set of explanations and a collection of facts, you could teach it with blackboard and chalk. You could assign students to read chapters and answer the questions that followed. Good students would take notes, read the text, turn in assignments, then give you all this information back again on a final exam. Science is traditionally taught in this manner. Everybody learns the same body of information at the same time. Class togetherness is preserved.

But science is more than this.

Science is also process — a dynamic interaction of rational inquiry and creative play. Scientists probe, poke, handle, observe, question, think up theories, test ideas, jump to conclusions, make mistakes, revise, synthesize, communicate, disagree and discover. Students can understand science as process only if they are free to think and act like scientists, in a classroom that recognizes and honors individual differences.

Science is *both* a traditional body of knowledge *and* an individualized process of creative inquiry. Science as process cannot ignore tradition. We stand on the shoulders of those who have gone before. If each generation reinvents the wheel, there is no time to discover the stars. Nor can traditional science continue to evolve and redefine itself without process. Science without this cutting edge of discovery is a static, dead thing.

Here is a teaching model that combines the best of both elements into one integrated whole. It is only a model. Like any scientific theory, it must give way over time to new and better ideas. We challenge you to incorporate this TOPS model into your own teaching practice. Change it and make it better so it works for you.

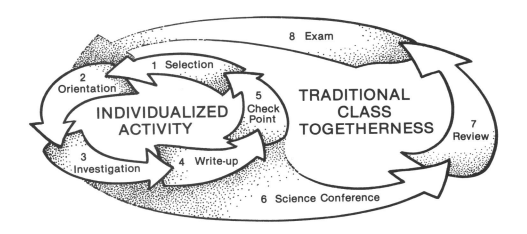

1. SELECTION

Doing TOPS is as easy as selecting the first task card and doing what it says, then the second, then the third, and so on. Working at their own pace, students fall into a natural routine that creates stability and order. They still have questions and problems, to be sure, but students know where they are and where they need to go.

Students generally select task cards in sequence because new concepts build on old ones in a specific order. There are, however, exceptions to this rule: students might *skip* a task that is not challenging; *repeat* a task with doubtful results; *add* a task of their own design to answer original "what would happen if" questions.

2. ORIENTATION

Many students will simply read a task card and immediately understand what to do. Others will require further verbal interpretation. Identify poor readers in your class. When they ask, "What does this mean?" they may be asking in reality, "Will you please read this card aloud?"

With such a diverse range of talent among students, how can you individualize activity and still hope to finish this module as a cohesive group? It's easy. By the time your most advanced students have completed all the task cards, including the enrichment series at the end, your slower students have at least completed the basic core curriculum. This core provides the common background so necessary for meaningful discussion, review and testing on a class basis.

3. INVESTIGATION

Students work through the task cards independently and cooperatively. They follow their own experimental strategies and help each other. You encourage this behavior by helping students only *after* they have tried to help themselves. As a resource person, you work to stay *out* of the center of attention, answering student questions rather than posing teacher questions.

When you need to speak to everyone at once, it is appropriate to interrupt individual task card activity and address the whole class, rather than repeat yourself over and over again. If you plan ahead, you'll find that most interruptions can fit into brief introductory remarks at the beginning of each new period.

4. WRITE-UP

Task cards ask students to explain the "how and why" of things. Write-ups are brief and to the point. Students may accelerate their pace through the task cards by writing these reports out of class.

Students may work alone or in cooperative lab groups. But each one must prepare an original write-up. These must be brought to the teacher for approval as soon as they are completed. Avoid dealing with too many write-ups near the end of the module, by enforcing this simple rule: each write-up must be approved *before* continuing on to the next task card.

5. CHECK POINT

The student and teacher evaluate each write-up together on a pass/no-pass basis. (Thus no time is wasted haggling over grades.) If the student has made reasonable effort consistent with individual ability, the write-up is checked off on a progress chart and included in the student's personal assignment folder or notebook kept on file in class.

Because the student is present when you evaluate, feedback is immediate and effective. A few seconds of this direct student-teacher interaction is surely more effective than 5 minutes worth of margin notes that students may or may not heed. Remember, you don't have to point out every error. Zero in on particulars. If reasonable effort has not been made, direct students to make specific improvements, and see you again for a follow-up check point.

A responsible lab assistant can double the amount of individual attention each student receives. If he or she is mature and respected by your students, have the assistant check the even-numbered write-ups while you check the odd ones. This will balance the work load and insure that all students receive equal treatment.

6. SCIENCE CONFERENCE

After individualized task card activity has ended, this is a time for students to come together, to discuss experimental results, to debate and draw conclusions. Slower students learn about the enrichment activities of faster students. Those who did original investigations, or made unusual discoveries, share this information with their peers, just like scientists at a real conference. This conference is open to films, newspaper articles and community speakers. It is a perfect time to consider the technological and social implications of the topic you are studying.

7. READ AND REVIEW

Does your school have an adopted science textbook? Do parts of your science syllabus still need to be covered? Now is the time to integrate other traditional science resources into your overall program. Your students already share a common background of hands-on lab work. With this shared base of experience, they can now read the text with greater understanding, think and problem-solve more successfully, communicate more effectively.

You might spend just a day on this step or an entire week. Finish with a review of key concepts in preparation for the final exam. Test questions in this module provide an excellent basis for discussion and study.

8. EXAM

Use any combination of the review/test questions, plus questions of your own, to determine how well students have mastered the concepts they've been learning. Those who finish your exam early might begin work on the first activity in the next new TOPS module.

Now that your class has completed a major TOPS learning cycle, it's time to start fresh with a brand new topic. Those who messed up and got behind don't need to stay there. Everyone begins the new topic on an equal footing. This frequent change of pace encourages your students to work hard, to enjoy what they learn, and thereby grow in scientific literacy.

GETTING READY

Here is a checklist of things to think about and preparations to make before your first lesson.

☐ Decide if this TOPS module is the best one to teach next.

TOPS modules are flexible. They can generally be scheduled in any order to meet your own class needs. Some lessons within certain modules, however, do require basic math skills or a knowledge of fundamental laboratory techniques. Review the task cards in this module now if you are not yet familiar with them. Decide whether you should teach any of these other TOPS modules first: *Measuring Length, Graphing, Metric Measure, Weighing* or *Electricity* (before *Magnetism*). It may be that your students already possess these requisite skills or that you can compensate with extra class discussion or special assistance.

☐ Number your task card masters in pencil.

The small number printed in the lower right corner of each task card shows its position within the overall series. If this ordering fits your schedule, copy each number into the blank parentheses directly above it at the top of the card. Be sure to use pencil rather than ink. You may decide to revise, upgrade or rearrange these task cards next time you teach this module. To do this, write your own better ideas on blank 4 x 6 index cards, and renumber them into the task card sequence wherever they fit best. In this manner, your curriculum will adapt and grow as you do.

☐ Copy your task card masters.

You have our permission to reproduce these task cards, for as long as you teach, with only 1 restriction: please limit the distribution of copies you make to the students you personally teach. Encourage other teachers who want to use this module to purchase their *own* copy. This supports TOPS financially, enabling us to continue publishing new TOPS modules for you. For a full list of task card options, please turn to the first task card masters numbered "cards 1-2."

☐ Collect needed materials.

Please see the opposite page.

☐ Organize a way to track completed assignment.

Keep write-ups on file in class. If you lack a vertical file, a box with a brick will serve. File folders or notebooks both make suitable assignment organizers. Students will feel a sense of accomplishment as they see their file folders grow heavy, or their notebooks fill up, with completed assignments. Easy reference and convenient review are assured, since all papers remain in one place.

Ask students to staple a sheet of numbered graph paper to the inside front cover of their file folder or notebook. Use this paper to track each student's progress through the module. Simply initial the corresponding task card number as students turn in each assignment.

☐ Review safety procedures.

Most TOPS experiments are safe even for small children. Certain lessons, however, require heat from a candle flame or Bunsen burner. Others require students to handle sharp objects like scissors, straight pins and razor blades. These task cards should not be attempted by immature students unless they are closely supervised. You might choose instead to turn these experiments into teacher demonstrations.

Unusual hazards are noted in the teaching notes and task cards where appropriate. But the curriculum cannot anticipate irresponsible behavior or negligence. It is ultimately the teacher's responsibility to see that common sense safety rules are followed at all times. Begin with these basic safety rules:

1. Eye Protection: Wear safety goggles when heating liquids or solids to high temperatures.
2. Poisons: Never taste anything unless told to do so.
3. Fire: Keep loose hair or clothing away from flames. Point test tubes which are heating away from your face and your neighbor's.
4. Glass Tubing: Don't force through stoppers. (The teacher should fit glass tubes to stoppers in advance, using a lubricant.)
5. Gas: Light the match first, before turning on the gas.

☐ Communicate your grading expectations.

Whatever your philosophy of grading, your students need to understand the standards you expect and how they will be assessed. Here is a grading scheme that counts individual effort, attitude and overall achievement. We think these 3 components deserve equal weight:

1. Pace (effort): Tally the number of check points you have initialed on the graph paper attached to each student's file folder or science notebook. Low ability students should be able to keep pace with gifted students, since write-ups are evaluated relative to individual performance standards. Students with absences or those who tend to work at a slow pace may (or may not) choose to overcome this disadvantage by assigning themselves more homework out of class.

2. Participation (attitude): This is a subjective grade assigned to reflect each student's attitude and class behavior. Active participators who work to capacity receive high marks. Inactive onlookers, who waste time in class and copy the results of others, receive low marks.

3. Exam (achievement): Task cards point toward generalizations that provide a base for hypothesizing and predicting. A final test over the entire module determines whether students understand relevant theory and can apply it in a predictive way.

Gathering Materials

Listed below is everything you'll need to teach this module. You already have many of these items. The rest are available from your supermarket, drugstore and hardware store. Laboratory supplies may be ordered through a science supply catalog. Hobby stores also carry basic science equipment.

Keep this classification key in mind as you review what's needed:

special in-a-box materials:	general on-the-shelf materials:
Italic type suggests that these materials are unusual. Keep these specialty items in a separate box. After you finish teaching this module, label the box for storage and put it away, ready to use again the next time you teach this module.	Normal type suggests that these materials are common. Keep these basics on shelves or in drawers that are readily accessible to your students. The next TOPS module you teach will likely utilize many of these same materials.
(substituted materials):	*optional materials:
A parentheses following any item suggests a ready substitute. These alternatives may work just as well as the original, perhaps better. Don't be afraid to improvise, to make do with what you have.	An asterisk sets these items apart. They are nice to have, but you can easily live without them. They are probably not worth the extra trip, unless you are gathering other materials as well.

Everything is listed in order of first use. Start gathering at the top of this list and work down. Ask students to bring recycled items from home. The teaching notes may occasionally suggest additional student activity under the heading "Extensions." Materials for these optional experiments are listed neither here nor in the teaching notes. Read the extension itself to find out what new materials, if any, are required.

Needed quantities depend on how many students you have, how you organize them into activity groups, and how you teach. Decide which of these 3 estimates best applies to you, then adjust quantities up or down as necessary:

$Q_1 / Q_2 / Q_3$

Single Student: Enough for 1 student to do all the experiments.
Individualized Approach: Enough for 30 students informally working in 10 lab groups, all self-paced.
Traditional Approach: Enough for 30 students, organized into 10 lab groups, all doing the same lesson.

KEY:	*special in-a-box materials* (substituted materials)	general on-the-shelf materials *optional materials

1/10/10	small graduated cylinders — 10 mL	1/10/10	dropper bottles each of: white vinegar, iodine, water and ammonia — see teaching notes 5 and 9 for details
1/1/1	jar of sand		
1/1/1	source of water		
1/10/10	Bunsen burners (an electric hot plate or warm radiator)	2/20/20	additional dropper bottles
		1/10/10	paper clips
2/20/20	Pyrex beakers — 50 to 100 mL capacity (crucibles or tuna fish cans)	1/1/1	roll aluminum foil
		1/10/10	candles with drip catchers (Bunsen burners or alcohol lamps)
2/20/20	watch glasses (tin can lids or crucibles or squares of cardboard)	5/10/5	baby food jars or equivalent
1/10/10	tongs (clothespins)	10/100/100	*strips each of red and blue litmus paper*
1/10/10	scissors	1/1/1	roll waxed paper
1/10/10	lab balances — those improvised in TOPS module *Weighing 05* are suitable	1/1/1	small portions each of *cleanser* and garden lime dispensed in labeled lids
1/1/1	*bottle sublimed sulfur*	1/10/10	*aspirin tablets*
5/50/50	*bottle caps*	1/10/10	straight pins
1/10/10	index cards	1/1/1	head red (purple) cabbage
1/1/1	roll masking tape	1/2/2	lemons (bottled concentrate or ascorbic acid crystals)
1/1/1	package: alum, baking soda, corn starch, salt and sugar; include a dispensing spoon with each box — see teaching notes 5	1/1/1	can beets — see teaching notes 15
		1/10/10	seltzer tablets

Sequencing Task Cards

This logic tree shows how all the task cards in this module tie together. In general, students begin at the trunk of the tree and work up through the related branches. As the diagram suggests, the way to upper level activities leads up from lower level activities.

At the teacher's discretion, certain activities can be omitted or sequences changed to meet specific class needs. The only activities that must be completed in sequence are indicated by leaves that open *vertically* into the ones above them. In these cases the lower activity is a prerequisite to the upper.

When possible, students should complete the task cards in the same sequence as numbered. If time is short, however, or certain students need to catch up, you can use the logic tree to identify concept-related *horizontal* activities. Some of these might be omitted since they serve only to reinforce learned concepts rather than introduce new ones.

On the other hand, if students complete all the activities at a certain horizontal concept level, then experience difficulty at the next higher level, you might go back down the logic tree to have students repeat specific key activities for greater reinforcement.

For whatever reason, when you wish to make sequence changes, you'll find this logic tree a valuable reference. Parentheses in the upper right corner of each task card allow you total flexibility. They are left blank so you can pencil in sequence numbers of your own choosing.

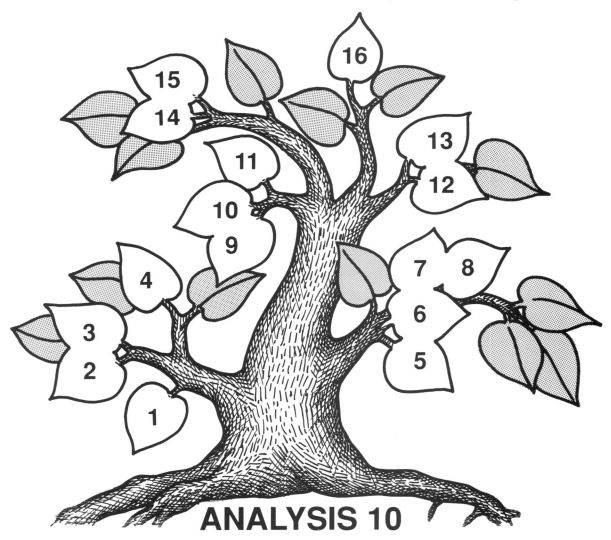

ANALYSIS 10

LONG-RANGE
OBJECTIVES

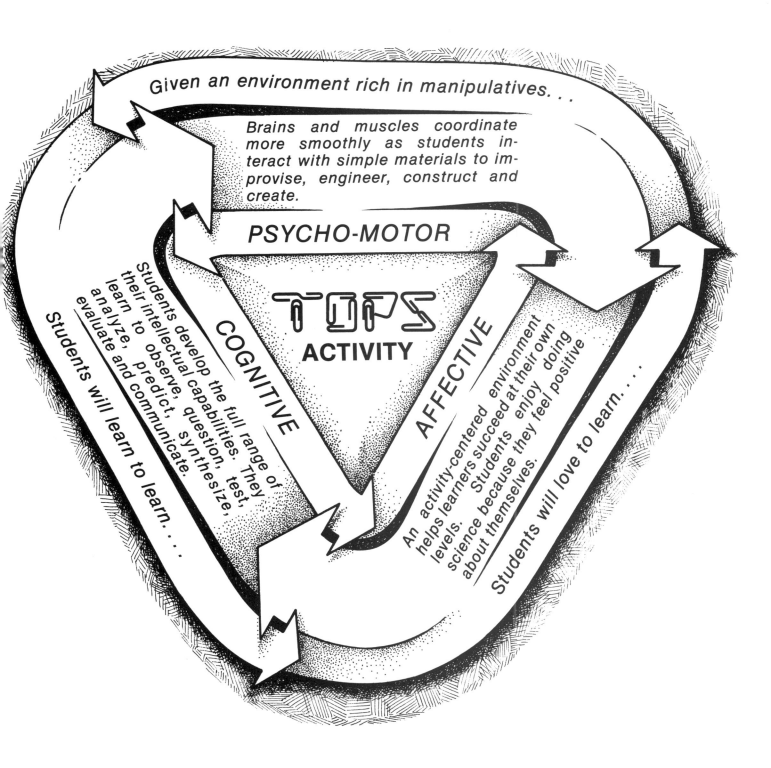

Given an environment rich in manipulatives. . .

Brains and muscles coordinate more smoothly as students interact with simple materials to improvise, engineer, construct and create.

PSYCHO-MOTOR

TOPS
ACTIVITY

COGNITIVE

Students develop the full range of their intellectual capabilities. They learn to observe, question, test, analyze, predict, synthesize, evaluate and communicate.

Students will learn to learn. . . .

AFFECTIVE

An activity-centered environment helps learners succeed at their own levels. Students enjoy doing science because they feel positive about themselves.

Students will love to learn. . . .

Review / Test Questions

Photocopy the questions below. On a separate sheet of blank paper, cut and paste those boxes you want to use as test questions. Include questions of your own design, as well. Crowd all these questions onto a single page for students to answer on another paper, or leave space for student responses after each question, as you wish. Duplicate a class set and your custom-made test is ready to use. Use leftover questions as a review in preparation for the final exam.

task 1-2
Consider this flow chart.

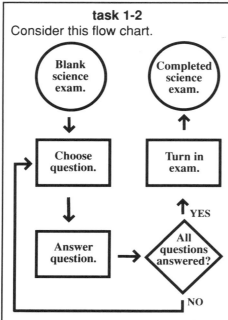

a. Why do the boxes have different shapes?
b. Why does the flow chart have a loop?

task 3-4
A mixture with a mass of 23.4 g was separated according to this flow chart, resulting in 15.3 g of sand.

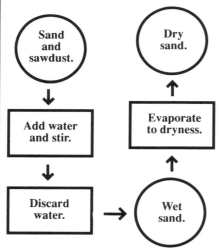

a. How much sawdust was in the mixture?
b. Name a source of error (other than errors in weighing) that might make this value too high.
c. Name a source of error (other than errors in weighing) that might make this value too low.

task 3-4
A student recorded the following data about the mass of a sample of Raisin Bran breakfast cereal:
  Raisin Bran in bowl = 238.9 g
       empty bowl = 203.2 g
           raisins = 15.0 g
Find the mass of the bran flakes.

task 3, 8
Distinguish between a quantitative analysis and a qualitative analysis.

task 4
Design a flow chart for separating a mixture of sand and iron filings with a magnet.

task 5
List the powders (alum, baking soda, corn starch, salt and/or sugar) that give positive reactions to each testing agent.
blackens with iodine:
fizzes with vinegar:
fizzes with baking soda water:
melts with heat:
burns with heat:

task 6-8
Which mixture of powders is harder to identify: sugar + salt, or corn starch + baking soda? Explain.

task 7-8
An unknown powder partially melts as it is heated, but it will not burn.
a. What *must* be in the mixture? Explain.
b. What *can't* be in the mixture? Explain.
c. What *might* be in the mixture? Explain.

task 9
Summarize how litmus paper responds to:
a. water.
b. ammonia.
c. vinegar.

task 10
Can basic ammonia be changed to acid by diluting it with water? Explain.

task 9-11
Both lemons and limes are highly acidic fruits. Propose an experiment using litmus paper to find which contains the stronger acid.

task 12-13
Cabbage water is added to a test tube of clear ammonia. The solution is then titrated drop by drop with vinegar until it turns highly acidic.
a. Describe the full range of color changes in the test tube as vinegar is added.
b. In what direction does the pH change in this test tube?

task 13-14
Cabbage water turns bluish green with baking soda, and pinkish purple with alum.
How would a mixture of these powders react with cabbage water? Explain.

task 13-14
Five solutions with pH's of 3,5,7,9 and 11 are placed in unlabeled glass vials. Can you order them from low pH to high pH…
a. using just litmus paper? Explain.
b. using just cabbage water? Explain.

task 15
Blueberry juice is known to change color in response to changing pH. How would you investigate its properties?

task 16
Aspirin dissolves in water to form an equilibrium of negative and positive ions.

$$AH \rightarrow A^- + H^+$$

How does this equilibrium respond if you…
a. Take away hydrogen ions by neutralizing with ammonia?
b. Add more hydrogen ions by acidifying with vinegar?

task 16
How might you compare commercial antacids (Rolaids and Tums, for example) to see which is the stronger buffer.

G

Answers

task 1-2
a. The boxes have different shapes because they have different functions: a circle tells you what you have, a rectangle tells you what to do, a diamond ask you to make a decision.
b. The flow chart loops to insure that that all questions are answered before the exam is turned in.

task 3-4
a.
$$\begin{aligned} \text{sand} + \text{sawdust} &= 23.4 \text{ g} \\ - \text{sand} &= \underline{15.3 \text{ g}} \\ \text{sawdust} &= 8.1 \text{ g} \end{aligned}$$

b. The sawdust will weigh too much if the sand weighs too little: perhaps part of the sand washed away with the sawdust, or was lost by splattering as it dried.
c. The sawdust will weigh too little if the sand weighs too much: perhaps sawdust remains with the sand in an incomplete separation, or moisture remains because the sand wasn't evaporated to complete dryness.

task 3-4
$$\begin{aligned} \text{Raisin Bran} + \text{bowl} &= 238.9 \text{ g} \\ - \text{bowl} &= \underline{203.2 \text{ g}} \\ \text{Raisin Bran} &= 35.7 \text{ g} \\ - \text{raisins} &= \underline{15.0 \text{ g}} \\ \text{bran flakes} &= 20.7 \text{ g} \end{aligned}$$

task 3, 8
A quantitative analysis is concerned with quantity — *how much* of this or that a mixture contains.
A qualitative analysis is concerned with quality — *what* a mixture contains.

task 4

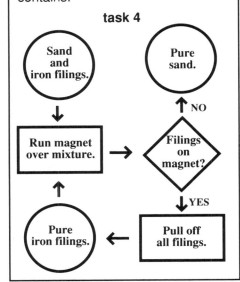

task 5
blackens with iodine: corn starch
fizzes with vinegar: baking soda
fizzes with baking soda water: alum
melts with heat: alum, sugar
burns with heat: corn starch, sugar

task 6-8
A mixture of sugar + salt is more difficult to identify. Neither react with iodine, vinegar or baking soda water. When heated, the sugar melts and burns into a puffy carbon crust that masks the presence of the inert salt.

A mixture of corn starch + baking soda, by contrast, is easy to identify because both have unique reactions: only corn starch blackens with iodine and only baking soda fizzes with vinegar.

task 7-8
a. Alum *must* be in the mixture because it is the only substance that melts but doesn't burn.
b. Sugar and corn starch *can't* be in the mixture, because both these substances would have burned.
c. Baking soda and salt *might* be in the mixture. Neither of these substances melts or burns.

task 9
a. water: Blue litmus stays blue and red litmus stays red.
b. ammonia: Blue litmus stays blue and red litmus changes blue.
c. acid: Blue litmus changes red and red litmus stays red.

task 10
No. Diluting ammonia (or any other base) only cuts its strength until it approaches that of water.

task 9-11
Place equal volumes of lemon juice and lime juice on waxed paper, forming two separate puddles. Then titrate each puddle, drop by drop, with ammonia, stirring all the time with a piece of red litmus paper. Note which puddle is the *last* to change the litmus paper to blue. This is the strongest acid.

task 12-13
a. The cabbage water starts out green-yellow because ammonia is strongly basic. It then neutralizes through green, green-blue and blue, then acidifies into purple, purple-pink, and finally into pink.
b. The pH continually drops as the solution changes from base to neutral to acid.

task 13-14
The powders would neutralize each other, producing a color between purple and blue.

task 13-14
a. Not completely. Litmus paper will identify two acids with low pH, the neutral solution with a pH of 7, and two bases with high pH. But it will not easily distinguish between the acids or bases to show which are stronger.
b. Yes. Each pH has its own corresponding color:
   pH = 3 (pink)
   pH = 5 (purple)
   pH = 7 (blue or greenish blue)
   pH = 9 (green or bluish green)
   pH = 11 (yellowish green)

task 15
Titrate several drops of blueberry juice with vinegar and note any color changes as the pH drops. Likewise, titrate another puddle of blueberry juice with ammonia and note any color changes as the pH rises.

task 16
a. The equilibrium shifts *right* to replace hydrogen ions that were neutralized by the ammonia.
b. The equilibrium shifts *left* to consume excess hydrogen ions that were added by the vinegar.

task 16
Weigh out equal portions of both antacids for a fair comparison, then thoroughly dissolve each in equal volumes of cabbage water. Now titrate equal portions of each dissolved antacid, first with vinegar, and then with ammonia. The sample that changes color most slowly will be the strongest buffer.

TEACHING NOTES
For Activities 1-16

Task Objective (TO) learn how to interpret flow chart instructions.

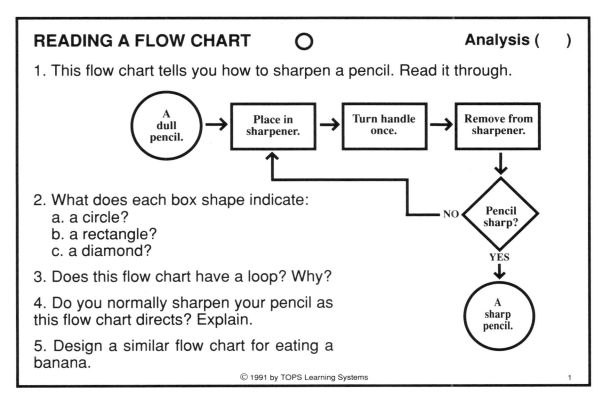

READING A FLOW CHART ○   Analysis ( )

1. This flow chart tells you how to sharpen a pencil. Read it through.

2. What does each box shape indicate:
   a. a circle?
   b. a rectangle?
   c. a diamond?

3. Does this flow chart have a loop? Why?

4. Do you normally sharpen your pencil as this flow chart directs? Explain.

5. Design a similar flow chart for eating a banana.

© 1991 by TOPS Learning Systems   1

Answers / Notes

2a. A circle tells you what you have.
2b. A rectangle tells you what to do.
2c. A diamond asks you to make a decision.

3. Yes. The pencil may not be sharp after only one turn of the handle. The "NO" track out of the decision box loops you back to the first command box, instructing you to give the handle another turn.

4. No. You normally don't take your pencil out of the sharpener to evaluate its sharpness after each turn of the handle.

5. Flow chart designs will vary. Here is one possible answer:

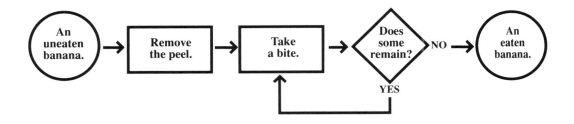

Materials

None required.

(TO) separate a mixture of salt and sand following flow chart directions.

SAND FROM SALT (1)　　○　　　　**Analysis (　)**

1. Mix sand and salt together in a heat resistant container as directed below. Follow this flow chart to separate them again.

```
Add 4 mL          A            Add 4 mL        Stir well
sand to    →   sand-salt   →    water.    →   with pencil.
4 mL salt.      mixture.

Cover loosely.                               
Evaporate   ←   Wet     ←   Pour off    →   Salt
to dryness.     sand.        liquid.        water.

   ↓                                          ↓

  Sand.                         Salt.   ←   Cover loosely.
                                            Evaporate
                                            to dryness.
```

2. Is your sand-salt separation complete? How do you know?

3. Save your container of salt-crusted sand for the next activity. You may discard the dingy salt.

2

Answers / Notes

1. *Caution students to keep their containers loosely covered, allowing evaporation, yet containing hot splatters. Splattering is especially severe near the end point as the last traces of moisture are driven off from the salt and sand.*

   Continue heating until all moisture disappears from the sides of the container and the lids. If you are heating over a gentle heat source, such as a school radiator, leave the containers in place to evaporate overnight.

2. No. The sand is covered by a white crust of salt, and the salt has a dingy off-white appearance compared to its original color.

Materials

☐ A dry 10 mL graduate. To dry a wet cylinder, wipe with a scrap of paper towel that is taped to the end of a straw.
☐ Sand.
☐ Table salt.
☐ A heat source. Use a Bunsen burner, electric hot plate or a warm radiator. Don't substitute candles. They don't deliver the required heat, and leave messy carbon deposits.
☐ Two heat resistant containers, plus coverings. Small Pyrex beakers, about 100 mL capacity, work best. You may substitute crucibles or tuna fish cans. Cover with watch glasses, pieces of cardboard, large tin can lids or perhaps a second crucible. Lids are optional if you use gentle radiator heating.
☐ A pair of tongs to handle the hot containers. Wooden clothespins also work if you caution students to squeeze the *edges* of the clothespin wings as shown. Otherwise, they may inadvertently drop their containers.
☐ A source of water.

YES:　　　　NO:

(TO) separate a mixture of salt and sand quantitatively, following flow chart directions.

SAND FROM SALT (2)　　　　○　　　　**Analysis (　)**

1. Gently break up your salt-crusted sand with the end of a pair of scissors. Follow this flow chart to make a complete separation.

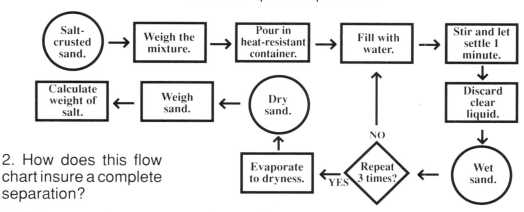

2. How does this flow chart insure a complete separation?

3. This separation was *quantitative*. The last one was not.
　　a. What is a quantitative separation?
　　b. What kind of experimental errors might give you MORE salt than you started with? LESS salt than you started with?

3

Answers / Notes

1. *Results will vary somewhat, depending on the starting masses of salt and sand. Here is one result:*

　　　mixture:　9.35 g
　　　　sand:　-5.16 g
　　　　salt:　　4.19 g

2. The flow chart loops to insure a complete separation. The wet sand is washed three times with large amounts of water.

3a. A quantitative separation keeps track of quantity: you find out *how much* sand and *how much* salt are in the mixture.

3b. The weight of the salt is calculated by subtracting the weight of the sand from the entire mixture.
　　More salt: any decrease in the sand's weight (lost during washing) increases this subtracted difference.
　　Less salt: any increase in the sand's weight (not evaporating to dryness) decreases this subtracted difference.

Materials

☐ Salt-crusted sand in its evaporating container, plus covering, used in the previous task card.
☐ A pair of scissors.
☐ A pair of tongs or a clothespin.
☐ A lab balance. The equal-arm balance constructed in *Weighing 05* is suitable to use here and in all TOPS experiments that require weight measure.
☐ A heat source.
☐ A source of water.

(TO) develop a flow chart for quantitatively separating sand and sulfur.

WRITE A FLOW CHART ○   Analysis ( )

1. Add a pinch of sand to a pinch of sulfur; mix thoroughly with your pencil. Try separating this mixture by repeatedly adding water. Can you do it?

SAND + SULFUR

2. Design a flow chart for *quantitatively* separating a mixture of sand and sulfur.

3. Thoroughly mix exactly 6.00 g of sand with 3.00 g of sulfur. Use this mixture to evaluate your flow-chart design and experimental accuracy.

4

Answers / Notes

1. Yes. Sulfur floats to the surface in water, while sand remains at the bottom.
   The sand-sulfur mixture needs repeated washings to insure a complete separation. Allow the sediments to settle before pouring off the floating sulfur. Otherwise lighter particles of sand may wash away with the sulfur.
2. *Encourage students to model their flow chart designs on the previous activity. Since this is a quantitative separation, the mixture must be initially weighed, so a subtraction can be made later. It is not necessary to save the sulfur.*

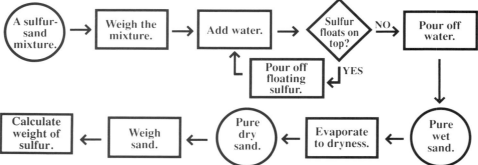

3.
mixture:	9.00 g
sand:	-5.91 g
sulfur:	3.09 g

The flow chart yielded quantitative answers, as designed, but the final mass of the sand was .09 g short of the expected 6.00 g. Apparently this much sand washed away during the rinsings. This error, in turn, resulted in a mass of the sulfur that was .09 g higher than the anticipated 3.00g.

Materials

☐ Sublimed (powdered) sulfur. Find this in the home remedy section of your local drug store. In its powdered form, sulfur floats, allowing an easy separation with water. Sawdust can be separated from sand in a similar manner and may be substituted.

☐ Sand.
☐ A heat resistant container, plus covering.
☐ A pair of tongs or a clothespin.
☐ A lab balance.
☐ A heat source.
☐ A source of water.

(TO) develop a reaction table to use as a reference for identifying unknown powders.

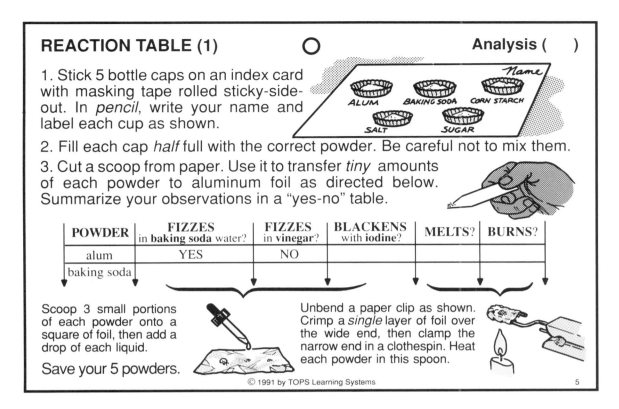

REACTION TABLE (1)   ○   Analysis ( )

1. Stick 5 bottle caps on an index card with masking tape rolled sticky-side-out. In *pencil*, write your name and label each cup as shown.

2. Fill each cap *half* full with the correct powder. Be careful not to mix them.

3. Cut a scoop from paper. Use it to transfer *tiny* amounts of each powder to aluminum foil as directed below. Summarize your observations in a "yes-no" table.

POWDER	FIZZES in **baking soda** water?	FIZZES in **vinegar**?	BLACKENS with **iodine**?	MELTS?	BURNS?
alum	YES	NO			
baking soda					

Scoop 3 small portions of each powder onto a square of foil, then add a drop of each liquid.

Save your 5 powders.

Unbend a paper clip as shown. Crimp a *single* layer of foil over the wide end, then clamp the narrow end in a clothespin. Heat each powder in this spoon.

© 1991 by TOPS Learning Systems   5

Answers / Notes

1. *This card must be labeled in pencil (not pen) because these labels will be revised in activities 7 and 8.*
3.

POWDER	FIZZES in **baking soda** water?	FIZZES in **vinegar**?	BLACKENS with **iodine**?	MELTS?	BURNS?
alum	YES	NO	NO	YES	NO
baking soda	NO	YES	NO	NO	NO
corn starch	NO	NO	YES	NO	YES
salt	NO	NO	NO	NO	NO
sugar	NO	NO	NO	YES	YES

Materials

□ Five bottle caps and an index card.
□ Masking tape.
□ Five white powders, plus dispensing spoons:
  •Alum. Find this aluminum salt in the home remedy section of your drug store.
  •Sodium bicarbonate, also called baking soda. Do *not* substitute baking powder.
  •Corn starch.
  •Salt. Select a brand with the smallest possible grain size. Some stores sell popcorn salt, which has smaller grains than refined table salt. Use this if available.
  •Granulated sugar. Again, select the smallest possible grain size. Use confectioners sugar if available, but *not* powdered sugar. Powdered sugars usually contain a corn starch additive.

□ Scissors.
□ Three clear liquids, dispensed in dropper bottles.
  •Baking soda water. Mix excess sodium bicarbonate in water and pour off the clear solution to use.
  •White distilled vinegar.
  •Tincture of iodine. The product sold in drug stores may be diluted up to 1 part in 99 parts water and still give a strong reaction if the solution is fresh. The dropper bottle should carry a warning label indicating that iodine is poisonous and will stain clothing. If you have iodine crystals and potassium iodide in stock, you can also make your own tincture according to this recipe: $2 \text{ g } I_2 + 5 \text{ g } KI + 1 \text{ liter } H_2O$.
□ A paper clip.
□ Aluminum foil.
□ A candle with drip catcher. Bunsen burners or alcohol lamps are also suitable.

(TO) react powders in combination and observe possible masking effects. To further refine a table of reactions to be used in identifying unknown powders.

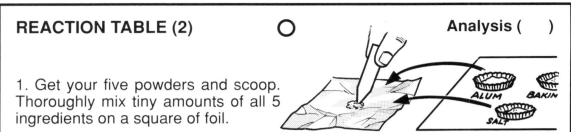

REACTION TABLE (2)   O   **Analysis (   )**

1. Get your five powders and scoop. Thoroughly mix tiny amounts of all 5 ingredients on a square of foil.

2. Test parts of your mixture with soda water, vinegar, iodine and heat.
   a. Which powders are easy to identify? Why?
   b. Which powders are more difficult? Why?

3. Refine your observations about each powder's reaction to heat beyond "yes" or "no." Use full, descriptive phrases.

POWDER	Reaction to **GENTLE HEAT** (Little or no burning.)	Reaction to **EXTREME HEAT**
alum		
baking soda		

4. Test your combination of 5 ingredients with gentle heat, then extreme heat. Which powders are easily identified and which are masked?

© 1991 by TOPS Learning Systems   6

Answers / Notes

2a. Three powders are relatively easy to identify because each has a unique reaction: soda water fizzes *only* with alum; vinegar fizzes *only* with baking soda; iodine turns black *only* with corn starch.

2b. Two powders are more difficult to identify. Sugar reacts strongly with heat. But so do other powders: alum melts and corn starch burns. Salt does not react at all, so its presence is masked by the presence of other powders. *(Students will discover in step 3 that salt does react subtly with extreme heat.)*

3.

POWDER	Reaction to **GENTLE HEAT** (Little or no burning.)	Reaction to **EXTREME HEAT**
alum	First melts, then forms large distinct bubbles.	Boils and crackles, then solidifies; will not burn.
baking soda	No reaction.	No reaction.
corn starch	Slowly browns, then blackens, while giving off smoke.	Ignites and rapidly burns. Does not puff up.
salt	No reaction.	The tiny grains tend to shatter and pop.
sugar	Melts easily, then boils, then gradually turns brown.	Turns carbon-black and puffs up; much smoke with a burned-sugar smell; may ignite.

4. Alum and sugar give strong, unique reactions with heat that are not readily masked by other powders. But the black puffs of burning sugar tend to mask the popping salt grains and slower, flat-burning cornstarch. The presence of baking soda is completely hidden, because it doesn't react at all. It must be identified with vinegar.

Materials

☐ The five powders assembled previously on an index card, plus paper scoop.
☐ The three clear testing liquids dispensed in dropper bottles.
☐ A flame source, plus matches.
☐ Aluminum foil and scissors.
☐ The paper-clip-and-foil spoon.

(TO) qualitatively analyze the composition of various mixtures of white powders, using testing agents that react in characteristic ways.

POWDER PUZZLES (1) ◯   Analysis (   )

1. Empty your bottle cap tray of all traces of powder. Erase each name and relabel as shown.

2. Refill each bottle cap with the correct mystery powder: 7A, 7B, 7C, 7D, 7E.

3. Use your reaction tables from the last two activities to find out what each powder contains. List all ingredients next to its label code, then answer the follow-up question:

(7A)_____. Did all ingredients melt? What does this rule out?
(7B)_____. Does a lack of reaction ever provide useful information?
(7C)_____. Can you be sure whether or not this sample contains salt?
(7D)_____. Can you be sure whether or not this sample contains salt?
(7E)_____. Was it really necessary to test this sample with heat?

7

Answers / Notes

3. *Aluminum foil that forms the spoon need not be replaced after each test. It can simply be wiped clean with a paper towel.*

(7A) alum, sugar: Yes. All ingredients melted before anything burned. This implies that the mixture cannot contain powders that don't melt (baking soda, cornstarch or salt).

(7B) salt: Yes. Negative reactions tell what the powder does not contain. Knowing what is not in the powder, by a process of elimination, indicates what is.

(7C) baking soda, salt: Yes. The salt grains crack and pop when subjected to extreme heat. This subtle reaction is not masked by baking soda, because it remains inert to heat.

(7D) alum, corn starch, sugar: No. The sample could conceivably contain salt, yet give an identical reaction. Its subtle popping reaction to extreme heat would be masked by the melting of sugar and alum, plus the burning of corn starch and sugar.

(7E) alum, baking soda, corn starch: Yes. In addition to the 3 powders revealed by the 3 test liquids, the mixture could have also contained salt and sugar. The heat test clearly eliminated the presence of sugar. The presence of salt is still in doubt. It could conceivable be present, but masked by the melting of alum and the burning of corn starch.

Materials

☐ Mystery powders labeled with the correct codes, 7A, 7B, etc., and formulated as detailed above. Thoroughly mix equal amounts of each ingredient in a labeled baby food jar or other small container in advance, away from student view.
☐ The bottle-cap organizing tray previously constructed, plus paper scoop.
☐ The three clear testing liquids dispensed in dropper bottles.
☐ A flame source, plus matches.
☐ Aluminum foil and scissors.
☐ Reaction tables from the previous 2 activities.
☐ The paper-clip-and-foil spoon.

(TO) continue analyzing the composition of various mixtures of white powder, using testing agents that react in characteristic ways.

POWDER PUZZLES (2) ◯   Analysis (   )

1. Empty your bottle cap tray again of all traces of powder. Erase each label, then relabel as shown.

2. Refill with a new set of mystery powders: 8A, 8B, 8C, 8D, 8E.

3. Qualitatively analyze each powder as before, listing ingredients and answering follow-up questions:

    (8A)_____. Sugar has a strong response to heat. Is this an advantage?
    (8B)_____. This mixture contains 1 or 2 powders. Is this a useful hint?
    (8C)_____. This mixture contains only 1 powder. Is this a useful hint?
    (8D)_____. Why does this compound fizz with iodine?
    (8E)_____. Salt is often masked by burning. Did this happen here?

4. How is this QUALitative analysis different from the QUANtitative analysis you did with salt, sulfur and sand?

© 1991 by TOPS Learning Systems   8

Answers / Notes

3.   (8A) baking soda, corn starch, sugar: No. Sugar is easy to identify when present, but it tends to mask the presence of other powders, especially salt.
    (8B) salt, sugar: No. Soda water, vinegar and iodine already confirm that the sample contains just 1 or 2 powders. The crucial question is whether this sample contains salt, which is easily masked by sugar.
    (8C) sugar: Yes. It is a very useful hint. Observing the positive heat test for sugar, the sample logically contains no salt nor other powder.
    (8D) alum, baking soda, corn starch, sugar: This mixture fizzes with iodine because its baking soda also dissolves in the tincture, producing soda water that reacts with its alum.
    (8E) alum, baking soda, salt: No. The mixture contained no powders that burned.

4. This qualitative analysis is concerned only with *what* a mixture contains. The previous quantitative analyses, by contrast, determined *how much*.

Materials

☐ Mystery powders labeled with the correct codes, 8A, 8B, etc., and formulated as detailed above. Thoroughly mix equal amounts of each ingredient in a labeled baby food jar or other small container in advance, away from student view.
☐ The bottle-cap organizing tray previously constructed, plus paper scoop.
☐ The three clear testing liquids dispensed in dropper bottles.
☐ A flame source, plus matches.
☐ Aluminum foil and scissors.
☐ Reaction tables from the previous 2 activities.
☐ The paper-clip-and-foil spoon.

(TO) discover how litmus paper responds to acids, bases and neutral solutions.

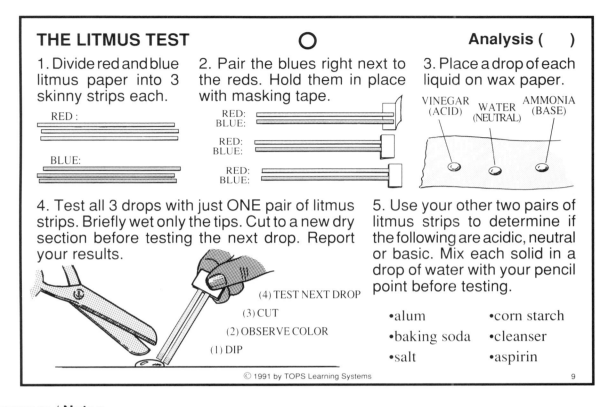

THE LITMUS TEST   ◯   Analysis (   )

1. Divide red and blue litmus paper into 3 skinny strips each.

RED:

BLUE:

2. Pair the blues right next to the reds. Hold them in place with masking tape.

RED:
BLUE:

RED:
BLUE:

RED:
BLUE:

3. Place a drop of each liquid on wax paper.

VINEGAR (ACID)   WATER (NEUTRAL)   AMMONIA (BASE)

4. Test all 3 drops with just ONE pair of litmus strips. Briefly wet only the tips. Cut to a new dry section before testing the next drop. Report your results.

(4) TEST NEXT DROP
(3) CUT
(2) OBSERVE COLOR
(1) DIP

5. Use your other two pairs of litmus strips to determine if the following are acidic, neutral or basic. Mix each solid in a drop of water with your pencil point before testing.

•alum   •corn starch
•baking soda   •cleanser
•salt   •aspirin

© 1991 by TOPS Learning Systems   9

Answers / Notes

4.

	vinegar (acid)	water (neutral)	ammonia (basic)
red litmus	red	red	blue
blue litmus	red	blue	blue

5. acids: aspirin, alum
neutral: salt, corn starch
bases: baking soda, cleanser

Materials

☐ A red and a blue litmus strip. Order these from any scientific supply store. Litmus strips can disappear as fast as chocolate candy if used indiscriminately. This activity (and others) runs on just one red strip and one blue strip per lab group.

☐ Scissors.

☐ Masking tape.

☐ Acid, neutral and base standards dispensed in dropper bottles labeled as underlined. Because future activities require uniform drop sizes for quantitative volumetric work, each lab group should have a dedicated set of three bottles. Tell students to identify their particular lab group on the label of each bottle.

   Vinegar (acid): fill dropper bottles with white distilled vinegar.

   Water (neutral): fill dropper bottles with tap water. If it is unusually acidic or basic, substitute distilled water.

   Ammonia (base): fill dropper bottles with clear household ammonia. Don't substitute brands that are colored with dyes or scented with other additives. Label the dropper bottle "poison." Caution students to avoid contact with eyes and skin, to rinse with water in case of accidental contact.

☐ Waxed paper. This works much better than plastic wrap.

☐ Alum, baking soda, corn starch and table salt from previous activities. These powders may be conveniently dispensed in the bottle cap tray first constructed in activity 5. But each cap must first be thoroughly cleaned and relabeled. Add sugar to its cap as well. Though it is not used in this activity, it will be required later.

☐ Kitchen cleanser. Dispense in a labeled lid or watch glass.

☐ Aspirin. Break whole tablets into quarters or eighths.

(TO) distinguish between water dilutions and acid-base neutralizations. To observe that the strength of an acid or base is reduced most effectively by neutralizing it.

DILUTE OR NEUTRALIZE? ◯   Analysis (   )

1. Cut and tape three pairs of thin red and blue litmus strips as before.

2. Add 4 separate drops of vinegar to a piece of wax paper. *Dilute* 3 of these drops with water as shown in the top table. Test each puddle with just *one* pair of litmus strips and record your results.

3. *Dilute* single drops of ammonia in the same manner. Record your results in the second table.

4. *Neutralize* each 2-drop portion of ammonia with vinegar. Complete the third table.

5. Water *dilutes,* but acids and bases *neutralize.*

   a. Did you change acid to base (or base to acid) by diluting with water? Explain.

   b. Did you change base to acid by neutralizing with acid? Explain.

DROPS OF VINEGAR	DROPS OF WATER	LITMUS RESPONSE?
1	0	
1	1	
1	5	
1	25	

DROPS OF AMMONIA	DROPS OF WATER	LITMUS RESPONSE?
1	0	
1	1	
1	5	
1	25	

DROPS OF AMMONIA	DROPS OF VINEGAR	LITMUS RESPONSE?
2	2	
2	3	
2	4	
2	5	

10

Introduction

Avoid contaminating one solution with another. Always allow the drop to fall cleanly away from the eyedropper *before* it makes contact with the target solution.

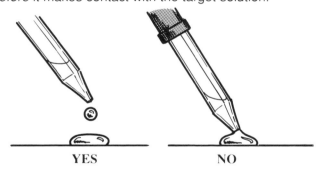

YES   NO

Materials

☐ A red and a blue litmus strip.
☐ Scissors.
☐ Masking tape.
☐ Vinegar, water and ammonia standards dispensed in dropper bottles.
☐ Waxed paper.

Answers / Notes

2.

DROPS OF VINEGAR	DROPS OF WATER	LITMUS RESPONSE?
1	0	red (acid)
1	1	red (acid)
1	5	red (acid)
1	25	red (acid)

3.

DROPS OF AMMONIA	DROPS OF WATER	LITMUS RESPONSE?
1	0	blue (base)
1	1	blue (base)
1	5	blue (base)
1	25	blue (base)

4.

DROPS OF AMMONIA	DROPS OF VINEGAR	LITMUS RESPONSE?
2	2	blue (base)
2	3	blue (base)
2	4	red (acid)
2	5	red (acid)

5a. No. Even when diluted by 25 drops of water, the vinegar remained acidic and the ammonia remained basic. Water may cut the strength of an acid or base, but it won't change one to the other.

5b. Yes. Two drops of ammonia was acidified with about four drops of vinegar.

(TO) compare the relative strengths of vinegar and ammonia by titrating with litmus paper.

TITRATION   O   Analysis ( )

1. Cut a small squares of red and blue litmus paper, then spindle them on a pin as shown:

2. Alternate drips of acid and base on waxed paper while you stir with the litmus squares.

    a. Will the same litmus papers change color back and forth? Report your findings.

    b. Can you bring the solution to neutral, between red and blue? Explain.

3. Count the drops of vinegar it takes to neutralize each quantity of ammonia, then calculate a ratio. Rinse the litmus squares in fresh water before each trial.

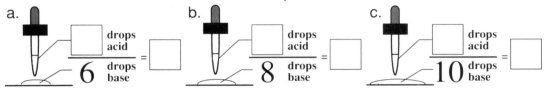

a. $\dfrac{\text{drops acid}}{6\ \text{drops base}} = \boxed{}$ b. $\dfrac{\text{drops acid}}{8\ \text{drops base}} = \boxed{}$ c. $\dfrac{\text{drops acid}}{10\ \text{drops base}} = \boxed{}$

4. Are your results consistent? Explain.

5. You have just *titrated* 3 times. Define what it means to titrate.

11

Answers / Notes

2a. Yes. The blue and red litmus squares turn red in vinegar, then change back to blue when this vinegar is neutralized by excess ammonia. This color change happens repeatedly as acid, then base, are alternatively added to the same puddle.

2b. Yes. If just enough ammonia is added to the vinegar, but not in excess, the litmus squares turn purple, halfway between red and blue. The same effect holds for adding just the right amount of vinegar to ammonia.

This neutral zone is somewhat elusive. Unless the puddle on the wax paper is quite large, a single drop of vinegar or ammonia is often enough to carry the solution beyond neutral into an acid red or basic blue. You can avoid overshooting by adding tiny amounts with the tip of your pencil.

3. *Answers will vary according to the strengths of the particular brands of vinegar and household ammonia you use. These ratios are further affected by the size of drops falling from each eyedropper. As long as lab groups consistently use the same two droppers, these drops don't need to be equal for experimental ratios to be in close agreement. Here is one set of results:*

$$\frac{\text{drops acid}}{\text{drops base}} = \overset{\text{a.}}{\frac{11}{6}} = \overset{\text{b.}}{\frac{15}{8}} = \overset{\text{c.}}{\frac{19}{10}} \approx 1.9$$

4. Yes. In each trial about 1.9 parts vinegar just neutralized 1 part ammonia, so that litmus papers remained in the purple range, halfway between red and blue.

5. To titrate means to neutralize a measured amount of acid with a measured amount of base (or base with acid) until an indicator changes color.

Materials

☐ A red and a blue litmus strip.
☐ Scissors.
☐ A straight pin.
☐ Vinegar, water and ammonia standards dispensed in dropper bottles.
☐ Waxed paper.
☐ A beaker or glass of rinse water.

(TO) investigate the properties of cabbage water as an acid-base indicator.

CABBAGE WATER INDICATOR ⬯   Analysis (　　)

1. Boil a few red cabbage leaves in a little water. Save the blue water in a labeled dropper bottle.

CABBAGE WATER

2. Place a drop of vinegar, water and ammonia on a piece of waxed paper backed by white paper. Evaluate how cabbage water responds as an acid-base indicator.

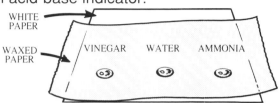

WHITE PAPER

WAXED PAPER

VINEGAR   WATER   AMMONIA

3. Use cabbage water to determine if each of the following is acid, neutral or base…

- garden lime ⎫
- sugar   ⎬ First dissolve in a drop of water; stir with pencil point.
- lemon juice ⎭

…Confirm your results with litmus paper.

4. Cabbage water spoils after several days, turning moldy and foul smelling. How might you make a cabbage indicator with a longer shelf life?

© 1991 by TOPS Learning Systems   12

Answers / Notes

2. Cabbage water turns …

   …PINK in acidic vinegar;   BLUE in neutral water;   GREEN-YELLOW in basic ammonia.

The neutral blue water drop gradually turns into basic green, as fumes from the adjacent ammonia drop slowly dissolve into it. Color observations here, and in activities to come, are somewhat time dependent.

3.   • Garden lime is basic: turns cabbage water green-yellow; turns red litmus blue.
     • Sugar is neutral: cabbage water remains purple; neither red nor blue litmus paper change color.
     • Lemon juice is acid: turns cabbage water pink; turns blue litmus red.

4. Soak sheets of paper towel in cabbage juice and allow them to dry. Then cut them into indicator strips to use like litmus paper. Or dry red cabbage leaves and grind them into a powder.

Extension

   Encourage students to explore their solutions to the spoilage problem posed in step 4. To inject a high concentration of blue cabbage dye into a paper towel, stand a small section upright in a beaker with juice that just covers the bottom. Capillary action draws the liquid up through the towel to the top edge where the water evaporates, leaving the dye behind.

PURPLE DYE

CABBAGE JUICE

Materials

☐ Red cabbage leaves. If you want your students to brew their own cabbage water, supply a Bunsen burner, alcohol lamp or hot plate, plus heat-resistant beaker and dropper bottle. Otherwise boil some up in advance and refrigerate. Distribute in labeled dropper bottles as required. Keep extra cabbage leaves on hand in case the liquid spoils before students finish this module.
☐ Vinegar, water and ammonia standards.
☐ Waxed paper.

☐ Garden lime. Use either a hydrated or dry form. The smallest package you can find, perhaps 5 pounds, will keep you supplied for the next 500 years.
☐ Sugar.
☐ Lemon juice. Use real lemons or bottled concentrate. Ascorbic acid crystals (vitamin C) may be substituted.
☐ A red and a blue litmus strip.
☐ Scissors.
☐ Masking tape.

(TO) examine the broad range of colors that cabbage water exhibits in response to acids and bases of various strengths.

COLOR RECIPES ◯   Analysis ( )

1. Put 5-drop puddles of cabbage water on waxed paper backed with white paper. Give recipes for adding ammonia or vinegar to produce these colors:

    a. pink   c. blue   e. green-yellow
    b. purple   d. green

(Split off tiny fractions of a drop as needed by tapping it with your pencil.)

2. The strength of an acid or base is measured in pH units. Low pH numbers indicate strong acids; high pH numbers, strong bases.

    a. Based on this chart, what is the pH of each solution you mixed?
    b. How do your color recipes support this chart? Explain.

ACID																BASE
	PINK		PINK purple		PURPLE pink		BLUE green		GREEN blue		GREEN yellow		YELLOW green			
	0	1	2	3	4	5 *PURPLE	6 *BLUE	7	8	9	10	11	12	13	14	
								neutral								
	PINK	PINK		PINK PURPLE		PURPLE blue		BLUE GREEN		GREEN		GREEN YELLOW		YELLOW		

© 1991 by TOPS Learning Systems   13

Answers / Notes.

1. *Red-green color blindness, partial or complete, is especially common among boys. Each lab group should have at least one color "expert" to assist those who are less color sensitive.*
1a. pink: add 4 or more drops of vinegar.
1b. purple: add nothing. This is the natural color of cabbage water.
1c. blue: add a tiny fraction of a drop of ammonia. *(This is the most elusive color. Much less than a drop of ammonia will shift 5 drops of purple cabbage water past true blue, into shades of green.)*
1d. green: add 2 drops of ammonia. *(One drop of our particular ammonia standard produced a green-tinted blue; three drops resulted in a green-tinted yellow.)*
1e. green-yellow: add 10 or more drops of ammonia. *(Deciding when a color is halfway between green and yellow is a subjective call.)*

2a. *There are no distinct end points in this color spectrum. Thus, pH values are only approximate.*
    pink: less than 3
    purple: between 5 and 6
    blue: between 6 and 7
    green: about 10
    green-yellow: about 12

2b. It took relatively more and more ammonia to shift purple cabbage water first to blue, then to green, then to green-yellow. As predicted by the pH chart, each of these colors is more basic than the one before. Likewise, vinegar was required to shift the purple cabbage water toward pink. This confirms that pink is where it belongs, on the acid side of the pH chart.

Materials

☐ Cabbage water.
☐ Waxed paper.
☐ Vinegar and ammonia.

(TO) estimate the pH of acids and bases by observing color changes in cabbage water. To confirm these results with litmus paper.

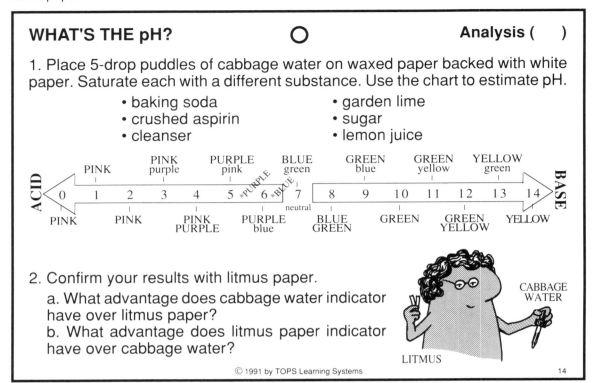

WHAT'S THE pH?   O   Analysis (   )

1. Place 5-drop puddles of cabbage water on waxed paper backed with white paper. Saturate each with a different substance. Use the chart to estimate pH.

- baking soda
- crushed aspirin
- cleanser

- garden lime
- sugar
- lemon juice

2. Confirm your results with litmus paper.
   a. What advantage does cabbage water indicator have over litmus paper?
   b. What advantage does litmus paper indicator have over cabbage water?

© 1991 by TOPS Learning Systems   14

Answers / Notes

1. *Expect considerable variation in pH values, depending on the amounts of powder actually dissolved in the cabbage water, and the somewhat subjective color calls of your students.*

- baking soda = 9
- crushed aspirin = 4
- cleanser = 10.5

- garden lime = 12
- sugar = 6-7
- lemon juice = less than 3

2. Litmus strips support the results in step 1: lemon juice and crushed aspirin tested acidic, turning blue litmus red; neither red nor blue litmus changed color with neutral sugar; baking soda, cleanser and garden lime all tested basic, turning red litmus blue.

2a. Cabbage water changes through a wide spectrum of color, indicating the relative strength of each acid or base. Litmus paper, by contrast, identifies that a solution is acid or base, but gives little indication of strength. *(Careful observers may notice that highly acidic solutions turn litmus a little more red and highly basic solutions turn litmus a more intense blue.)*

2b. Students may report that litmus paper is more convenient, easier to use, etc. Its most important advantage, however, is that it doesn't change the pH of the solution it measures. By contrast, cabbage water is a mildly acidic liquid. It raises the pH of lemon juice, for example, and lowers the pH of baking soda.

Materials

☐ Waxed paper.
☐ Cabbage water.
☐ Lemon juice. This is most conveniently dispensed with an eyedropper.
☐ Five powders: baking soda, crushed aspirin, cleanser, garden lime and sugar.
☐ A red and blue litmus strip.

(TO) study how beet juice interacts with acids and bases. To correlate its color change with pH.

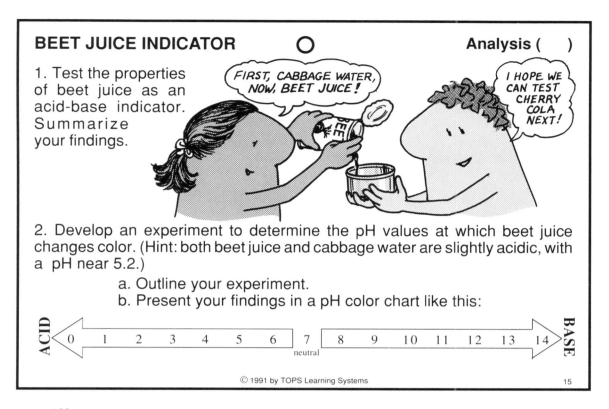

BEET JUICE INDICATOR ○   **Analysis ( )**

1. Test the properties of beet juice as an acid-base indicator. Summarize your findings.

FIRST, CABBAGE WATER, NOW, BEET JUICE!

I HOPE WE CAN TEST CHERRY COLA NEXT!

2. Develop an experiment to determine the pH values at which beet juice changes color. (Hint: both beet juice and cabbage water are slightly acidic, with a pH near 5.2.)

      a. Outline your experiment.
      b. Present your findings in a pH color chart like this:

ACID ← | 0 | 1 | 2 | 3 | 4 | 5 | 6 | 7 | 8 | 9 | 10 | 11 | 12 | 13 | 14 | → BASE

neutral

15

Answers / Notes

1. A drop of beet juice on waxed paper remains red with vinegar, but turns dark red to purple with ammonia. It is sensitive, therefore, to bases but not to acids.

2a. Students should titrate beet juice with ammonia until it just changes color, then add the same number of drops to cabbage water. The corresponding color change in cabbage water can then be correlated with its color chart to estimate the pH of the beet juice. Two problems, however, must be overcome.

First, the ammonia is much too strong, turning beet juice darker towards purple at the first drop. We found a 5% solution (5 drops ammonia diluted with 95 drops water) to be an ideal strength, producing color changes in a 5-drop puddle of beet juice after the third drop.

Second, the color changes are gradual. It is best to deposit a series of drops on waxed paper, each one containing a drop more of diluted ammonia than the one before. Subtle color changes are thus easier to recognize because colors can be compared, like beads on a necklace.

2b.

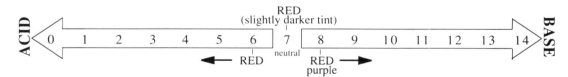

RED
(slightly darker tint)

ACID ← | 0 | 1 | 2 | 3 | 4 | 5 | 6 | 7 | 8 | 9 | 10 | 11 | 12 | 13 | 14 | → BASE

← RED   neutral   RED →
purple

Materials

☐ A can of beets. Read the label before purchasing. They must *not* be pickled (acidified with vinegar). Avoid accidental stains by dispensing the juice in dropper bottles.
☐ Cabbage water, pure water, ammonia and vinegar all dispensed in dropper bottles.
☐ Waxed paper.
☐ A jar or beaker and an eyedropper.
☐ A pH color chart (optional). Photocopy this from the supplementary page at the back of this book. (One sheet will serve 8 students.) Or, have students sketch their own versions.

(TO) observe how buffered solutions neutralize both excess acid and base to maintain a stable pH.

BUFFERS RESIST CHANGE ○   Analysis ( )

1. Dissolve a seltzer tablet in just a little water.

2. Pair puddles of this solution next to water on waxed paper as shown. Add 5 drops of cabbage water to all four puddles.

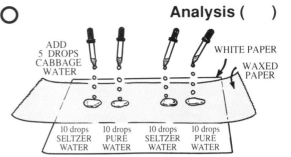

ADD 5 DROPS CABBAGE WATER

WHITE PAPER

WAXED PAPER

10 drops SELTZER WATER   10 drops PURE WATER   10 drops SELTZER WATER   10 drops PURE WATER

3. Now add vinegar, drop by drop, to one seltzer puddle and one water puddle. Which is *buffered* (resists changing)? How do you know?

4. Add ammonia, drop by drop, to the other pair of puddles. Does the same buffer also resist changing to base? Explain.

5. Ammonia and garden lime are both bases because they contain OH⁻ ions. Notice that one solution is in equilibrium while the other has gone to completion.

    a. How would you expect the pH of ammonia and garden lime to change as you add excess vinegar?

    b. Test your prediction.

ammonia:
$$NH_3 \rightleftharpoons NH_4^+ + OH^-$$

garden lime:
$$CaO + H_2O \rightarrow Ca^{++} + OH^-$$

© 1991 by TOPS Learning Systems

16

Introduction

Water in two jars is connected by a common tube. If you stir either jar, water molecules that shift right are replaced by others that shift left. But there is no net change. The jars of water are in *equilibrium*.

$$L \rightleftharpoons R$$

a. What happens when you add water to the right jar? (Water shifts left to relieve this stress, establishing a new higher equilibrium.)

b. What happens when you remove water from the right jar? (Water shifts right to relieve this stress, establishing a new lower equilibrium.)

Solutions that have hydrogen ions (H⁺) or hydroxide ions (OH⁻) in equilibrium are called buffers. Add acid (H⁺ ions) to a buffer, and its equilibrium shifts to neutralize it. Add base (OH⁻ ions) to this same buffer, and its equilibrium shifts the opposite way, again to neutralize.

Consider the vinegar buffer system: $VH \rightleftharpoons V^- + H^+$

a. How does this equilibrium shift when you add more hydrogen ions? (To the left, rejoining excess hydrogen ions to form whole vinegar molecules.)

b. How does this equilibrium shift when you add base (OH⁻)? (To the right, replacing H⁺ ions that were neutralized to water: $H^+ + OH^- \longrightarrow H_2O$.)

Answers / Notes

3. The seltzer solution is buffered. It changes from purple to pink (decreasing pH) more slowly than water.

4. Yes. Seltzer water changes through purple, blue, green and yellow (increasing pH) more slowly than water.

5a. H⁺ ions in the vinegar will neutralize OH⁻ ions in both solutions. But only ammonia, in equilibrium, can replenish its OH⁻ ions by shifting right. Its color should change towards acid more gradually than garden lime which has gone to completion.

5b. As predicted, garden lime shifted to purple with only 2 drops of vinegar. Buffered ammonia required about 18 drops of vinegar to shift to a similar color.

Materials

☐ A seltzer tablet. Use Alka-Seltzer or other buffered antacid.
☐ A jar or beaker and an eyedropper.
☐ Cabbage water, pure water, ammonia and vinegar all dispensed in dropper bottles.

notes 16   enrichment

REPRODUCIBLE
STUDENT
TASK CARDS

Task Cards Options

Here are 3 management options to consider before you photocopy:

1. Consumable Worksheets: Copy 1 complete set of task card pages. Cut out each card and fix it to a separate sheet of boldly lined paper. Duplicate a class set of each worksheet master you have made, 1 per student. Direct students to follow the task card instructions at the top of each page, then respond to questions in the lined space underneath.

2. Nonconsumable Reference Booklets: Copy and collate the 2-up task card pages in sequence. Make perhaps half as many sets as the students who will use them. Staple each set in the upper left corner, both front and back to prevent the outside pages from working loose. Tell students that these task card booklets are for reference only. They should use them as they would any textbook, responding to questions on their own papers, returning them unmarked and in good shape at the end of the module.

3. Nonconsumable Task Cards: Copy several sets of task card pages. Laminate them, if you wish, for extra durability, then cut out each card to display in your room. You might pin cards to bulletin boards; or punch out the holes and hang them from wall hooks (you can fashion hooks from paper clips and tape these to the wall); or fix cards to cereal boxes with paper fasteners, 4 to a box; or keep cards on designated reference tables. The important thing is to provide enough task card reference points about your classroom to avoid a jam of too many students at any one location. Two or 3 task card sets should accommodate everyone, since different students will use different cards at different times.

READING A FLOW CHART   O   Analysis (   )

1. This flow chart tells you how to sharpen a pencil. Read it through.

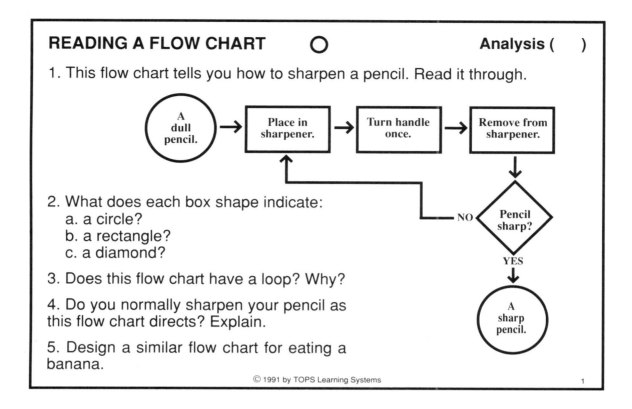

2. What does each box shape indicate:
   a. a circle?
   b. a rectangle?
   c. a diamond?

3. Does this flow chart have a loop? Why?

4. Do you normally sharpen your pencil as this flow chart directs? Explain.

5. Design a similar flow chart for eating a banana.

1

SAND FROM SALT (1)   O   Analysis (   )

1. Mix sand and salt together in a heat resistant container as directed below. Follow this flow chart to separate them again.

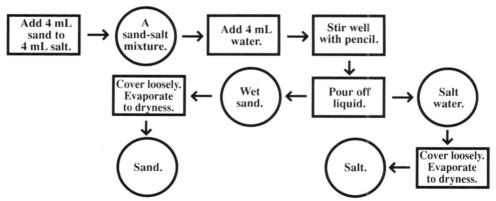

2. Is your sand-salt separation complete? How do you know?

3. Save your container of salt-crusted sand for the next activity. You may discard the dingy salt.

2

SAND FROM SALT (2) O Analysis (   )

1. Gently break up your salt-crusted sand with the end of a pair of scissors. Follow this flow chart to make a complete separation.

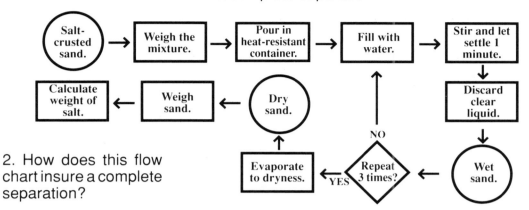

2. How does this flow chart insure a complete separation?

3. This separation was *quantitative*. The last one was not.
   a. What is a quantitative separation?
   b. What kind of experimental errors might give you MORE salt than you started with? LESS salt than you started with?

© 1991 by TOPS Learning Systems

3

WRITE A FLOW CHART O Analysis (   )

1. Add a pinch of sand to a pinch of sulfur; mix thoroughly with your pencil. Try separating this mixture by repeatedly adding water. Can you do it?

SAND + SULFUR

2. Design a flow chart for *quantitatively* separating a mixture of sand and sulfur.

3. Thoroughly mix exactly 6.00 g of sand with 3.00 g of sulfur. Use this mixture to evaluate your flow-chart design and experimental accuracy.

© 1991 by TOPS Learning Systems

4

REACTION TABLE (1)   O   Analysis (   )

1. Stick 5 bottle caps on an index card with masking tape rolled sticky-side-out. In *pencil*, write your name and label each cup as shown.

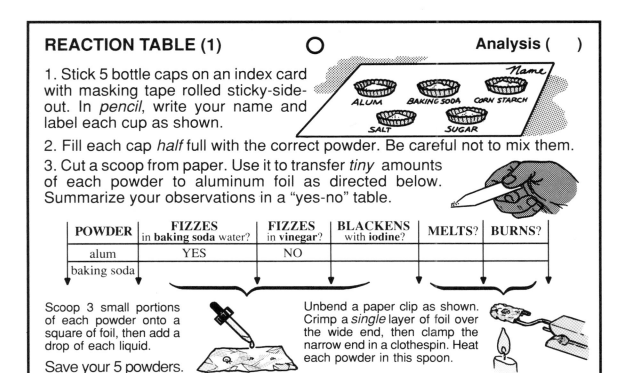

2. Fill each cap *half* full with the correct powder. Be careful not to mix them.

3. Cut a scoop from paper. Use it to transfer *tiny* amounts of each powder to aluminum foil as directed below. Summarize your observations in a "yes-no" table.

POWDER	FIZZES in **baking soda** water?	FIZZES in **vinegar**?	BLACKENS with **iodine**?	MELTS?	BURNS?
alum	YES	NO			
baking soda					

Scoop 3 small portions of each powder onto a square of foil, then add a drop of each liquid.

Save your 5 powders.

Unbend a paper clip as shown. Crimp a *single* layer of foil over the wide end, then clamp the narrow end in a clothespin. Heat each powder in this spoon.

5

REACTION TABLE (2)   O   Analysis (   )

1. Get your five powders and scoop. Thoroughly mix tiny amounts of all 5 ingredients on a square of foil.

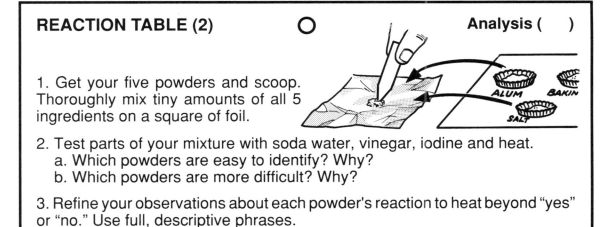

2. Test parts of your mixture with soda water, vinegar, iodine and heat.
   a. Which powders are easy to identify? Why?
   b. Which powders are more difficult? Why?

3. Refine your observations about each powder's reaction to heat beyond "yes" or "no." Use full, descriptive phrases.

POWDER	Reaction to **GENTLE HEAT** (Little or no burning.)	Reaction to **EXTREME HEAT**
alum		
baking soda		

4. Test your combination of 5 ingredients with gentle heat, then extreme heat. Which powders are easily identified and which are masked?

6

POWDER PUZZLES (1) ◯   Analysis (   )

1. Empty your bottle cap tray of all traces of powder. Erase each name and relabel as shown.

2. Refill each bottle cap with the correct mystery powder: 7A, 7B, 7C, 7D, 7E.

3. Use your reaction tables from the last two activities to find out what each powder contains. List all ingredients next to its label code, then answer the follow-up question:

    (7A)_____. Did all ingredients melt? What does this rule out?
    (7B)_____. Does a lack of reaction ever provide useful information?
    (7C)_____. Can you be sure whether or not this sample contains salt?
    (7D)_____. Can you be sure whether or not this sample contains salt?
    (7E)_____. Was it really necessary to test this sample with heat?

     7

POWDER PUZZLES (2) ◯   Analysis (   )

1. Empty your bottle cap tray again of all traces of powder. Erase each label, then relabel as shown.

2. Refill with a new set of mystery powders: 8A, 8B, 8C, 8D, 8E.

3. Qualitatively analyze each powder as before, listing ingredients and answering follow-up questions:

    (8A)_____. Sugar has a strong response to heat. Is this an advantage?
    (8B)_____. This mixture contains 1 or 2 powders. Is this a useful hint?
    (8C)_____. This mixture contains only 1 powder. Is this a useful hint?
    (8D)_____. Why does this compound fizz with iodine?
    (8E)_____. Salt is often masked by burning. Did this happen here?

4. How is this QUALitative analysis different from the QUANtitative analysis you did with salt, sulfur and sand?

     8

THE LITMUS TEST   ○   Analysis (   )

1. Divide red and blue litmus paper into 3 skinny strips each.

RED:

BLUE:

2. Pair the blues right next to the reds. Hold them in place with masking tape.

RED:
BLUE:

RED:
BLUE:

RED:
BLUE:

3. Place a drop of each liquid on wax paper.

VINEGAR (ACID)   WATER (NEUTRAL)   AMMONIA (BASE)

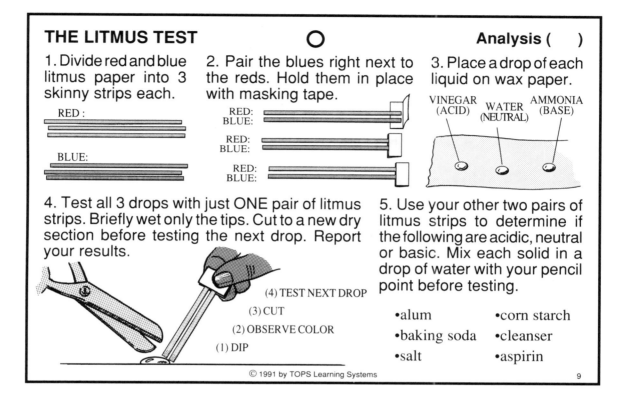

4. Test all 3 drops with just ONE pair of litmus strips. Briefly wet only the tips. Cut to a new dry section before testing the next drop. Report your results.

(4) TEST NEXT DROP
(3) CUT
(2) OBSERVE COLOR
(1) DIP

5. Use your other two pairs of litmus strips to determine if the following are acidic, neutral or basic. Mix each solid in a drop of water with your pencil point before testing.

- alum
- baking soda
- salt
- corn starch
- cleanser
- aspirin

9

DILUTE OR NEUTRALIZE?   ○   Analysis (   )

1. Cut and tape three pairs of thin red and blue litmus strips as before.

2. Add 4 separate drops of vinegar to a piece of wax paper. *Dilute* 3 of these drops with water as shown in the top table. Test each puddle with just *one* pair of litmus strips and record your results.

3. *Dilute* single drops of ammonia in the same manner. Record your results in the second table.

4. *Neutralize* each 2-drop portion of ammonia with vinegar. Complete the third table.

5. Water *dilutes,* but acids and bases *neutralize.*

   a. Did you change acid to base (or base to acid) by diluting with water? Explain.

   b. Did you change base to acid by neutralizing with acid? Explain.

DROPS OF VINEGAR	DROPS OF WATER	LITMUS RESPONSE?
1	0	
1	1	
1	5	
1	25	

DROPS OF AMMONIA	DROPS OF WATER	LITMUS RESPONSE?
1	0	
1	1	
1	5	
1	25	

DROPS OF AMMONIA	DROPS OF VINEGAR	LITMUS RESPONSE?
2	2	
2	3	
2	4	
2	5	

10

TITRATION ○ Analysis (   )

1. Cut a small squares of red and blue litmus paper, then spindle them on a pin as shown:

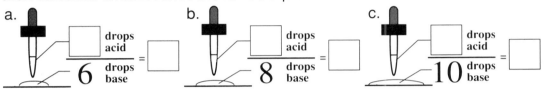

BLUE RED ACID BASE STIR

2. Alternate drips of acid and base on waxed paper while you stir with the litmus squares.

   a. Will the same litmus papers change color back and forth? Report your findings.

   b. Can you bring the solution to neutral, between red and blue? Explain.

3. Count the drops of vinegar it takes to neutralize each quantity of ammonia, then calculate a ratio. Rinse the litmus squares in fresh water before each trial.

a.
$$\dfrac{\text{drops acid}}{6 \text{ drops base}} = \boxed{}$$

b.
$$\dfrac{\text{drops acid}}{8 \text{ drops base}} = \boxed{}$$

c.
$$\dfrac{\text{drops acid}}{10 \text{ drops base}} = \boxed{}$$

4. Are your results consistent? Explain.

5. You have just *titrated* 3 times. Define what it means to titrate.

11

CABBAGE WATER INDICATOR ○ Analysis (   )

1. Boil a few red cabbage leaves in a little water. Save the blue water in a labeled dropper bottle.

CABBAGE WATER

2. Place a drop of vinegar, water and ammonia on a piece of waxed paper backed by white paper. Evaluate how cabbage water responds as an acid-base indicator.

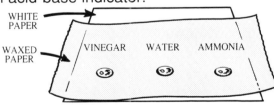

WHITE PAPER

WAXED PAPER

VINEGAR   WATER   AMMONIA

3. Use cabbage water to determine if each of the following is acid, neutral or base...

   • garden lime } First dissolve in a drop of water; stir with pencil point.
   • sugar
   • lemon juice

...Confirm your results with litmus paper.

4. Cabbage water spoils after several days, turning moldy and foul smelling. How might you make a cabbage indicator with a longer shelf life?

12

COLOR RECIPES ○   Analysis (   )

1. Put 5-drop puddles of cabbage water on waxed paper backed with white paper. Give recipes for adding ammonia or vinegar to produce these colors:

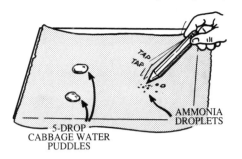

5-DROP CABBAGE WATER PUDDLES

AMMONIA DROPLETS

TAP TAP

    a. pink   c. blue   e. green-yellow
    b. purple   d. green

(Split off tiny fractions of a drop as needed by tapping it with your pencil.)

2. The strength of an acid or base is measured in pH units. Low pH numbers indicate strong acids; high pH numbers, strong bases.

    a. Based on this chart, what is the pH of each solution you mixed?
    b. How do your color recipes support this chart? Explain.

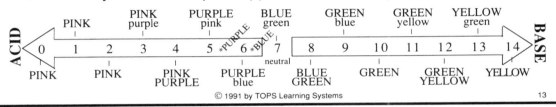

ACID ←——————————————————————————→ BASE

PINK | PINK purple | PURPLE pink | BLUE green | GREEN blue | GREEN yellow | YELLOW green

0 1 2 3 4 5 *PURPLE 6 *BLUE 7 8 9 10 11 12 13 14

neutral

PINK | PINK | PINK PURPLE | PURPLE blue | BLUE GREEN | GREEN | GREEN YELLOW | YELLOW

© 1991 by TOPS Learning Systems   13

WHAT'S THE pH? ○   Analysis (   )

1. Place 5-drop puddles of cabbage water on waxed paper backed with white paper. Saturate each with a different substance. Use the chart to estimate pH.

    • baking soda   • garden lime
    • crushed aspirin • sugar
    • cleanser   • lemon juice

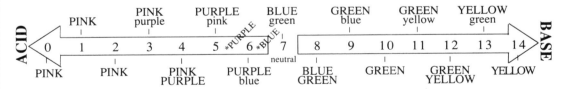

ACID ←——————————————————————————→ BASE

PINK | PINK purple | PURPLE pink | BLUE green | GREEN blue | GREEN yellow | YELLOW green

0 1 2 3 4 5 *PURPLE 6 *BLUE 7 8 9 10 11 12 13 14

neutral

PINK | PINK | PINK PURPLE | PURPLE blue | BLUE GREEN | GREEN | GREEN YELLOW | YELLOW

2. Confirm your results with litmus paper.

    a. What advantage does cabbage water indicator have over litmus paper?
    b. What advantage does litmus paper indicator have over cabbage water?

CABBAGE WATER

LITMUS

© 1991 by TOPS Learning Systems   14

---

cards 13-14

BEET JUICE INDICATOR ○ Analysis ( )

1. Test the properties of beet juice as an acid-base indicator. Summarize your findings.

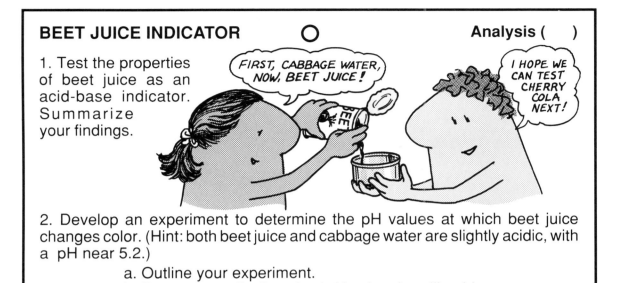

2. Develop an experiment to determine the pH values at which beet juice changes color. (Hint: both beet juice and cabbage water are slightly acidic, with a pH near 5.2.)

      a. Outline your experiment.
      b. Present your findings in a pH color chart like this:

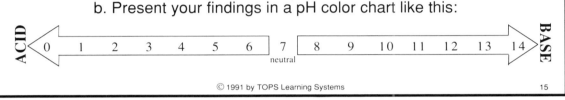

15

BUFFERS RESIST CHANGE ○ Analysis ( )

1. Dissolve a seltzer tablet in just a little water.

2. Pair puddles of this solution next to water on waxed paper as shown. Add 5 drops of cabbage water to all four puddles.

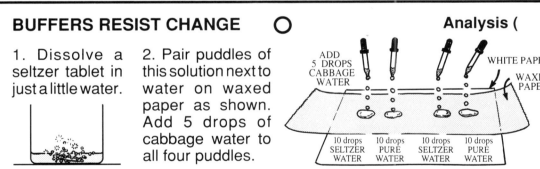

3. Now add vinegar, drop by drop, to one seltzer puddle and one water puddle. Which is *buffered* (resists changing)? How do you know?

4. Add ammonia, drop by drop, to the other pair of puddles. Does the same buffer also resist changing to base? Explain.

5. Ammonia and garden lime are both bases because they contain OH^- ions. Notice that one solution is in equilibrium while the other has gone to completion.

    a. How would you expect the pH of ammonia and garden lime to change as you add excess vinegar?
    b. Test your prediction.

ammonia:
$$NH_3 \rightleftharpoons NH_4^+ + OH^-$$

garden lime:
$$CaO + H_2O \rightarrow Ca^{++} + OH^-$$

16

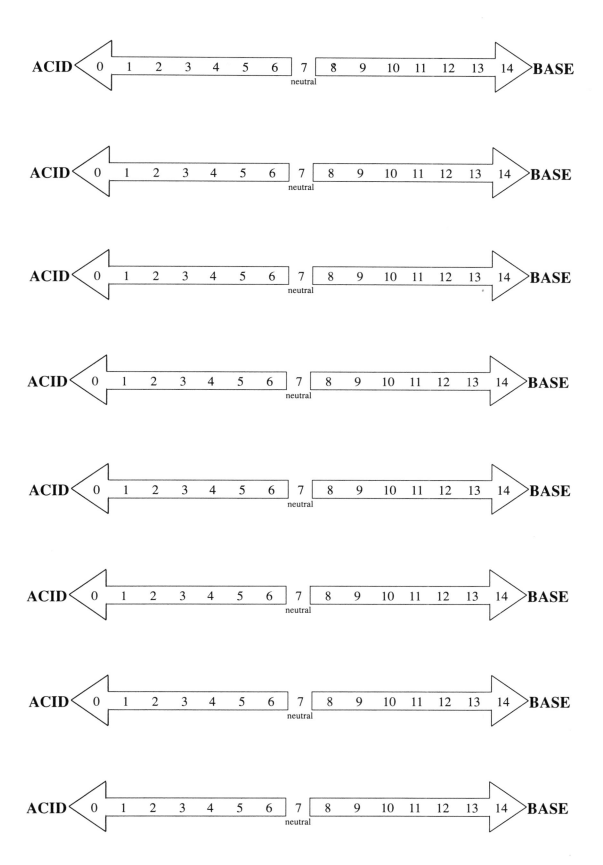